BIBLE MEN AND WOMEN FROM A TO Z

is a collection of rhymes and puzzles about Old Testament women and men, arranged alphabetically. Each rhyme is followed by a question about the biblical personality, which can be answered by looking up the Scripture reference given. Puzzles include crosswords, mazes, and word searches. Again, the answers are found by reading the Bible. This book is not only an educational tool, it is a learning activity and an entertaining game.

Designed for use in the home, Christian schools, and Sunday schools, **BIBLE MEN AND WOMEN FROM A TO Z** encourages children to read the Bible and helps them learn to use Scripture references. Through these activities, children, parents, and teachers will meet many fascinating characters. In finding answers to the questions, or working the varied types of puzzles, children will use every book of the Bible at least once! (Note: For a few letters, no proper name could be found in either Testament. In that case, a significant word has been chosen for the rhyme and question.) Occasionally you may need to check more than one version of the Bible. The two main versions used in preparing this book were The New International Version and The New Revised Standard Version.

The heroes in many of our books seem never to do anything wrong. Our Bible is a very unusual book in that its heroes and heroines are not perfect! God wants us to know that even when we make a mistake, God still loves us and cares for us.

A Note for Parents and Teachers

If your children are new to Bible study, show them the table of contents in their Bibles, where they can look up the beginning pages of the less familiar books. Talk about the division of each book into chapters and verses, then try some of the rhymes and questions.

You'll soon see many ways this activity booklet can be used. For instance you can make a game of finding the answers. You might also develop reading skills by asking children to read the verse or verses that answer the question. You can go back through the rhymes and questions again later, finding out more about the person named by reading some of the verses before and after the reference.

After using the activity for a while, make a game of answering the questions without reference to the Scripture verse!

1

AARON has two A's in his name,
But that is not his claim to fame.

Who was Aaron's famous brother?

_____

Leviticus 16:1-2

2

ABIGAIL was really pretty.
She was smart and also witty.

What was the name of Abigail's nasty husband?

_____

1 Samuel 25:3

3

AGABUS said, "Paul I do fear,
What will happen to you if you stay here."

What did Agabus do to show his fear?

_____

Acts 21:10-11

4

An evil man was **AHAB.**
He did things that made God mad.

Whose vineyard did Ahab want?

_____

1 Kings 21:1-2

UZZIAH ✰ AGABUS ☾ COZBI ✳ DAVID ✰

ZIPPORAH

TITUS ☾

UZZIAH

A Bible-Skills Activity Book

Bible

MEN & WOMEN

from

A to Z

REHOBOAM ✰

PAUL ✳

EPAPHRAS ☾ EZEKIEL ✳ FESTUS ✰ JESUS ☾

Rhymes, Questions, and Puzzles

Rosemary Frantz

Ages 7-11

☾ LOIS ✳ NEHEMIAH ✳ JOHANNA ☾

BIBLE MEN & WOMEN FROM A TO Z

Copyright © 1999 by Abingdon Press

Credits: p. 8 art: Robert S. Jones, © 1997 Abingdon Press; p. 9 art: Barbara Upchurch, © 1995 Cokesbury; p. 10 art: Jason Schreer, © 1995 Cokesbury; p. 11 art: Tom Armstrong © 1995 Cokesbury; p. 12 art: Charles Jakubowski, © 1998 Abingdon Press; p. 13 art: Robert S. Jones, © 1997 Abingdon Press; p. 16 art: Jim Padgett, © 1997 Abingdon Press; p. 17 art: Buford Winfrey, © 1995 Cokesbury; p. 18 art: Robert S. Jones, © 1998 Abingdon Press; p. 19 art: Susan Harrison, © 1995 Cokesbury; p. 20 art: Tom Dunnington/John Walter and Associates, © 1995 Cokesbury; p. 23 art: Robert S. Jones, © 1997 Abingdon Press; p. 31 © 1995 Cokesbury; p. 32 word find © 1998 Abingdon Press; p. 33 art: Charles Cox, © 1995 Cokesbury; p. 37 art: Buford Winfrey, © 1997 Abingdon Press; p. 38 art: Robert S. Jones, © 1997 Abingdon Press; p. 42 art: Brenda Gilliam, © 1994 Cokesbury; p. 45 art: Jack Kershner, © 1995 Cokesbury; p. 46 art: Corbin Hillam, © 1996 Cokesbury; p. 47 art: Doug Jones, © 1996 Cokesbury; p. 50 art: Bill Woods (map) and Barbara Upchurch (crossword), map © 1987 Graded Press, crossword © 1996 Cokesbury; p. 51 © 1996 Cokesbury; p. 54 art: Doug Jones, © 1998 Abingdon Press; p. 55 art: Jason Schreer, © 1995 Cokesbury; p. 60 art: Brenda Gilliam, © 1995 Cokesbury; p. 66 art: Lyn Martin, © 1996 Cokesbury.

ISBN 0-687-08344-3

99 00 01 02 03 04 05 06 07 08—10 9 8 7 6 5 4 3 2 1

MANUFACTURED IN THE UNITED STATES OF AMERICA

5
Images of Nature
In the Book of Amos

Amos was a shepherd. When God sent him to speak to
the people of Israel, he used many images from nature
to prophecy to the people. Find the images in the word search below.

```
F  W  I  L  D  E  R  N  E  S  S  L  D
R  I  O  M  O  U  N  T  A  I  N  A  U
U  A  G  R  A  I  N  E  N  I  R  M  S
I  H  O  R  S  E  S  E  V  K  O  B  T
T  H  G  I  L  E  D  O  N  O  O  I  H
H  G  R  D  D  R  R  E  N  F  T  R  T
K  L  A  A  A  Y  S  L  I  O  N  D  R
M  I  E  G  O  S  D  I  R  A  I  N  A
N  L  S  H  E  A  V  E  S  K  N  R  E
P  C  E  D  A  R  S  Q  C  S  O  P  O
```

FRUIT	**PLEADES**	**LION**
MOUNTAIN	**OAKS**	**LAMB**
EARTH	**ROOT**	**BIRD**
RAIN	**DUST**	**SHEAVES**
DARKNESS	**GRAIN**	**GARDEN**
WILDERNESS	**CEDARS**	**IVORY**
FIG	**HORSES**	
ORION		

6

ANNA was a very old lady
When God let her see his Holy Baby.

How old was Anna?

_____

Luke 2:25-38

7

Paul's letter says:
"Please aid and equip
friends Zenas and **APOLLOS**
for a very long trip."

Who was the lawyer, Zenas or Apollos?

_____

Titus 3:13

8

BALAAM's donkey would not obey;
The angel of the Lord was in her way.

What four things did Balaam's donkey do?

_____

_____

_____

Numbers 22:23, 25, 27-28

9

Paul and **BARNABAS** went to Jerusalem.
Their good friend Titus went along with them.

Why did Paul and Barnabas go to Jerusalem?

_____

Galatians 2:1-2

10

BATHSHEBA was a beautiful queen.
Her son, Solomon,
Became a wise king.

Who was the father of Bathsheba's son?

_____

1 Kings 2:1

11

One thousand people came to the feast,
BELSHAZZAR turned white when he saw a hand like a beast.

What did the giant hand do?
Who told the king what it meant?

_____

_____

Daniel 5:1-29

12

BERNICE came to the audience hall
To see and hear a man named Paul.

What was the name of the king who was with Bernice?

_____

Acts 25:13, 22-24

Use your Bible to meet some Bible families.

Example: Ruth 4:13-16

Ruth	Boaz
Parent	Parent

Obed
Child

Ruth
Parent

Obed
Child

Boaz
Parent

Naomi
Grand
Mother

Genesis 21:1-3

Parent	Parent

child

Genesis 25:19-21, 24-26

Parent	Parent

| child | child |

Exodus 2:1-10; Numbers 26:59

Parent	Parent

Pharaoh's Daughter

| child | child | child |

Luke 1:57-60

Parent	Parent

Child

Children are a blessing and a gift from the Lord.
Psalm 127:3 (CEV)

Why are families important?
How do you know that you are loved?
Who helps you grow in faith?
at home _____
_____
at church _____

2 Timothy 1:1-2, 5

Mother	Grandmother

Child

14

Circle of Bible Friends

The story of David and Jonathan is the best known story about friends in the Bible. However, there are other friends in the Bible.

As you find each one, write the names in the circle.

1 Samuel 19:1-2
(1. _____) took great delight in (2. _____).

James 2:23
(3. _____) was called the friend of God.

Job 2:11
(4. _____), (5. _____), and (6. _____)
were Job's three friends.

John 11:1-6, 11
Jesus considered (7. _____) and his two
sisters (8. ____) and (9. _____) his friends.

15

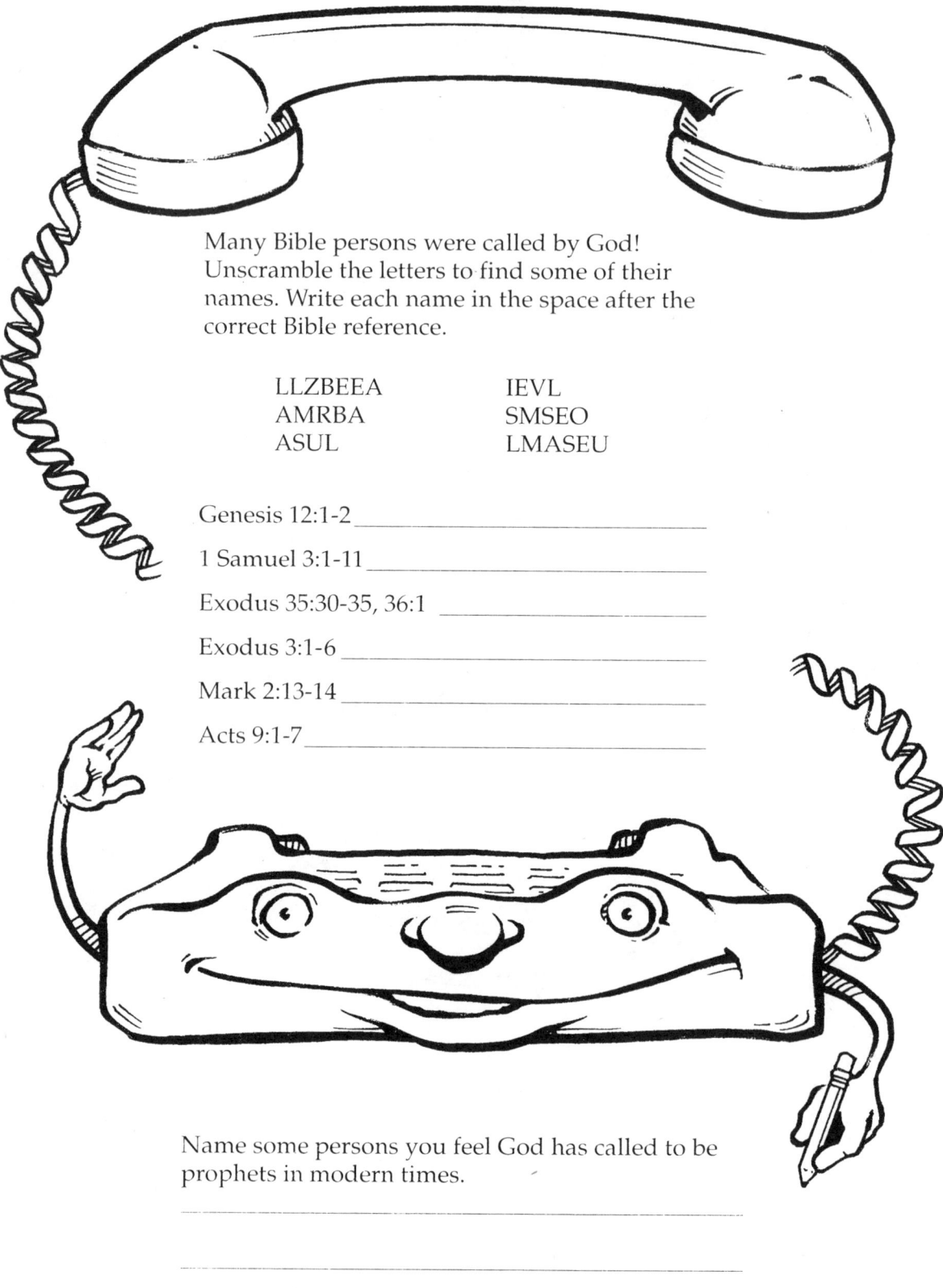

Many Bible persons were called by God! Unscramble the letters to find some of their names. Write each name in the space after the correct Bible reference.

LLZBEEA   IEVL
AMRBA   SMSEO
ASUL   LMASEU

Genesis 12:1-2 _____

1 Samuel 3:1-11 _____

Exodus 35:30-35, 36:1 _____

Exodus 3:1-6 _____

Mark 2:13-14 _____

Acts 9:1-7 _____

Name some persons you feel God has called to be prophets in modern times.

_____

_____

_____

16

Discover the names of some Bible persons who prayed.

Across

2. Prayed for the men who had been chosen to help feed the widows. (Acts 6:1-6)
4. Prayed that God would remember his faithfulness and not let him die from a deadly disease. (2 Kings 20:2-5)
5. Prayed to be saved from the belly of a fish. (Jonah 2:1-10)
7. Prayed that God's will be done rather than his own. (Matthew 26:36, 39)
9. Prayed to be freed from slavery in Egypt. (Exodus 2:23-25)

Down

1. Prayed that God would forgive the people who stoned him to death. (Acts 7:59-60)
3. Prayed for a sign that he would be successful in delivering Israel. (Judges 6:36-40)
6. Prayed for God to give her a son. (1 Samuel 1:7b-11)
8. Prayed for the people after they had sinned by speaking against God. (Numbers 21:7)

When do you pray?

17

In the patriarchal times of the Bible, women excelled in many occupations in addition to those of wife and mother. Find the Bible references to discover the names of professional women and businesswomen in Bible times.

Patriarchal means that families, tribes, and countries were ruled by men.

(Hebrew) _____
(Greek) _____
Disciple — Acts 9:36

_____
Tentmaker — Acts 18:1-3

_____
Prophet — Exodus 15:20

_____
Prophet — 2 Kings 22:12-14

_____
Missionaries — Philippians 4:2-3

_____
Judge — Judges 4:4-5

_____
Merchant — Acts 16:14

_____
Deacon — Romans 16:1

Read about a kind man's treatment of Ruth in Ruth 2:1-23.
Then complete the description of the man.

A KIND MAN

Name (Ruth 2:1) _____

Kinsman of (Ruth 2:1) _____

Financial Status (Ruth 2:1) _____

Occupation (Ruth 2:3) _____

Actions Toward Ruth

Told her to _____ only his fields. (Ruth 2:8)

Praised her loyalty to her mother-in-law, _____ . (Ruth 2:6, 11-12)

Said, "May the Lord _____ you for your _____ . (Ruth 2:12a)

Shared his _____ with her. (Ruth 2:14)

Instructed the reapers to leave _____ of grain for her to gather. (Ruth 2:15-16)

When Naomi heard what happened, she said of him, "_____ be the man who took notice of you." (Ruth 2:19)

Now write a post card to Boaz telling him what you have learned about being kind to others from his actions.

19

CALEB walked and walked all over the land.
The land God gave him was very grand.

How old was Caleb when the land was finally
given to him?

_____

Joshua 14:10-12

20

CLAUDIA helped the apostle Paul
Work and work and give his all.

Who, besides Claudia, sent greetings?

_____

2 Timothy 4:19-21

21

CLEMENT'S name is in the book of life.
He went to heaven, where there is no strife.

Who were the women who worked with Clement?

_____

Philippians 4:2-3

22

COZBI led an Israelite man astray.
She made him worship her god one day.

What was Cozbi's father named?

_____

Numbers 25:15

23

A king of Persia named **CYRUS**
Put his thoughts upon papyrus.

How many years had Cyrus been king when he wrote
these thoughts?

_____

Ezra 1:1

24

DANIEL told the king
what he wanted to know.
God gave him the words
so long, long ago.

What was the name of the king who wanted Daniel's advice?

_____

Daniel 2:25-28

25

Daniel and his friends were faithful to God by observing
the dietary laws of their Hebrew religion.
How did God bless them? (Read Daniel 1:17)

**1= A   2= D   3= E   4= G   5= H   6= I   7= K   8= L
9= M   10= N   11= O   12= R   13= S   14= T   15= U   16= W**

God gave them _____
 7 10 11 16 8 3 2 4 3

and _____ in every aspect of
 13 7 6 8 8

_____ and
 8 6 14 3 12 1 14 15 12 3

_____ .
 16 6 13 2 11 9

To Daniel, God also gave _____
 6 10 13 6 4 5 14

into all visions and dreams.

Daniel's Faithfulness

My Faithfulness

I was faithful when _____

_____

_____ .

God has blessed me by _____

_____ .

26

Read the Bible verses to help you fill in the blanks to complete the story. Then mark the map to show where David ruled.

Read 2 Samuel 2:1-4a
After Saul died, David became the king of _____ , the southern part of the kingdom.

Draw lines like these ////////// across the map to show where David ruled.

When David ruled in Judah, his capital city was _____ .

Draw a square around the dot that marks that city.

Read 2 Samuel 5:1-3
The tribes of Israel came to David at Hebron and asked him to rule over _____ also, the northern part of the kingdom.

Draw lines like these - - - - - across the map to show the Northern Kingdom.

Color the entire United Kingdom of Israel yellow.

Read 2 Samuel 5:6-7
When David ruled the United Kingdom, he moved his capital to

_____

Put a Star of David ✡ around the dot that marks that city.

Read 2 Samuel 5:4-5
David ruled as king of Judah for _____ years and _____ months.

Then David ruled as king of the United Kingdom for _____ years.

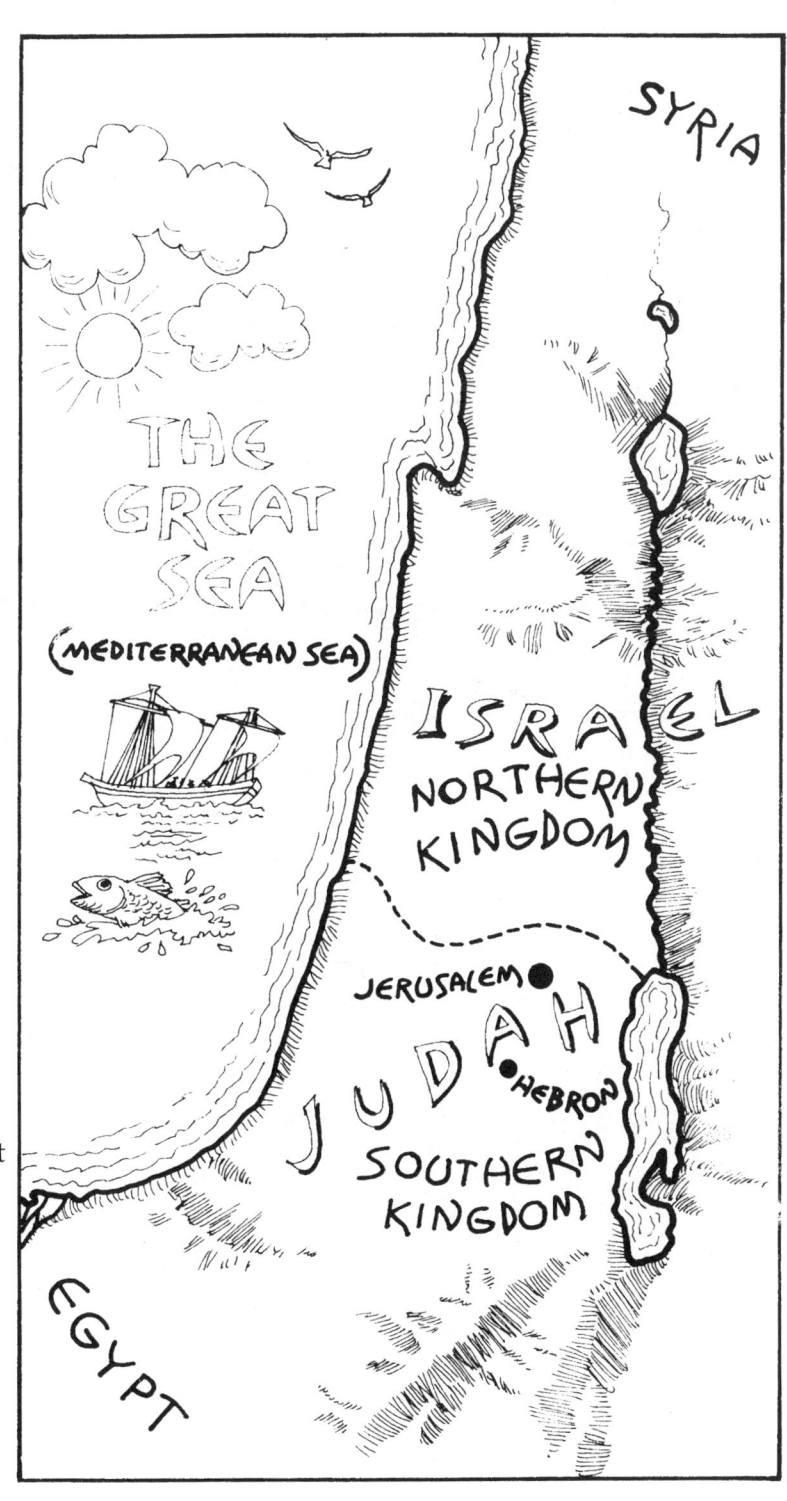

ACROSS

1. The city that became the capital city of the kingdom united under King David (2 Samuel 5:6-7, 9-10)
5. The king who felt better when David played music for him (1 Samuel 16:23)
7. David's hometown (1 Samuel 17:12)
8. The ark that contained the Ten Commandments was called the ark of _____ (2 Samuel 6:1-5)
9. A musical instrument played by David (1 Samuel 16:23)

DOWN

1. David's best friend (1 Samuel 18:1)
2. A woman who helped make peace when her husband refused to honor David (1 Samuel 25:23-25, 32-35)
3. Jonathan's son who was welcomed into King David's home (2 Samuel 9:3, 5-7)
4. The southern part of the kingdom where David first became king (2 Samuel 2:4a).
6. David's father (1 Samuel 16:11-12)

28

David made promises to Jonathan and Mephibosheth. Can you use the code to find each promise?

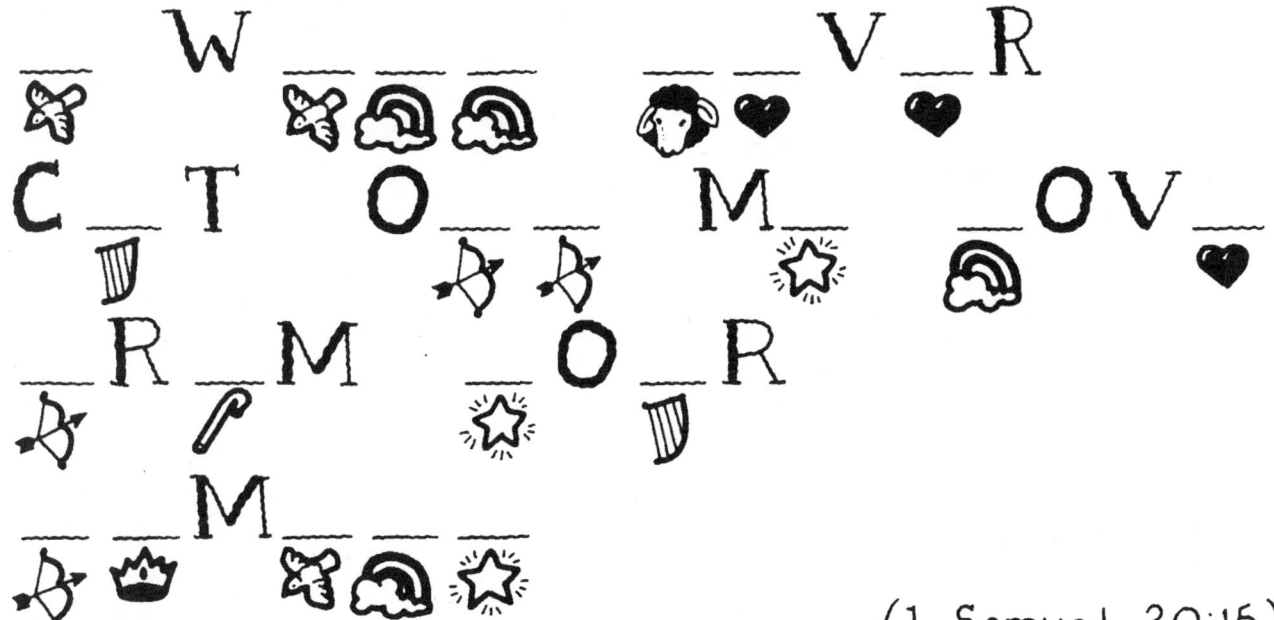

A E F I L N O U Y

Promise to Jonathan

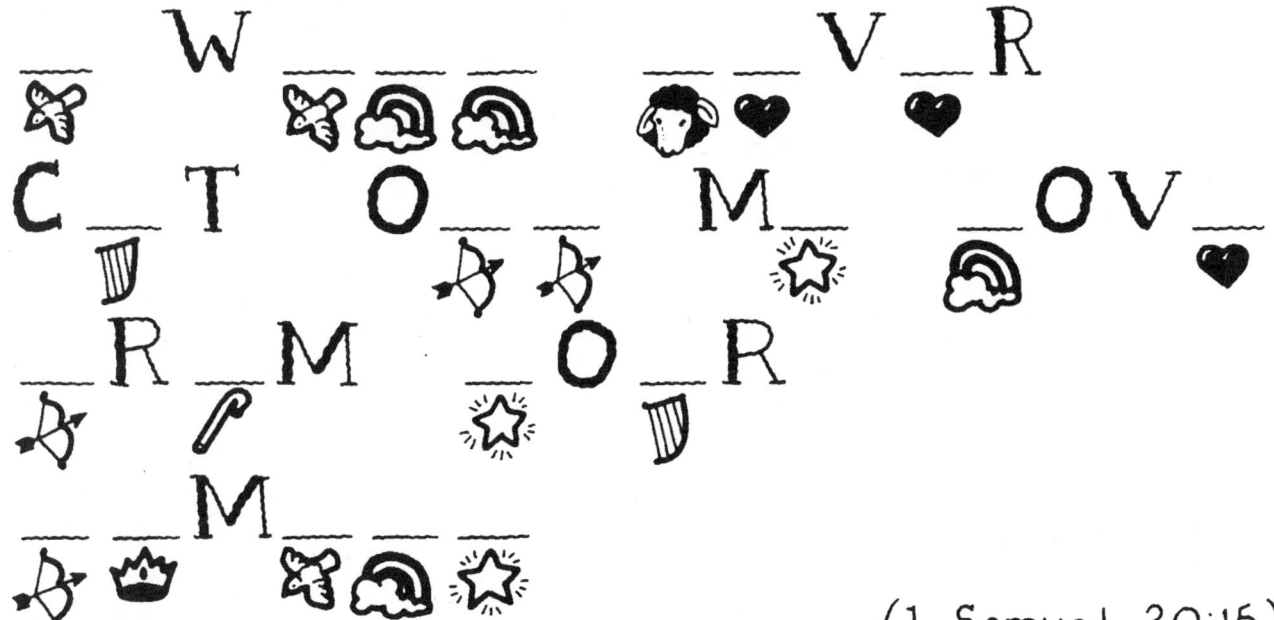

(1 Samuel 20:15)

Promise to Mephibosheth

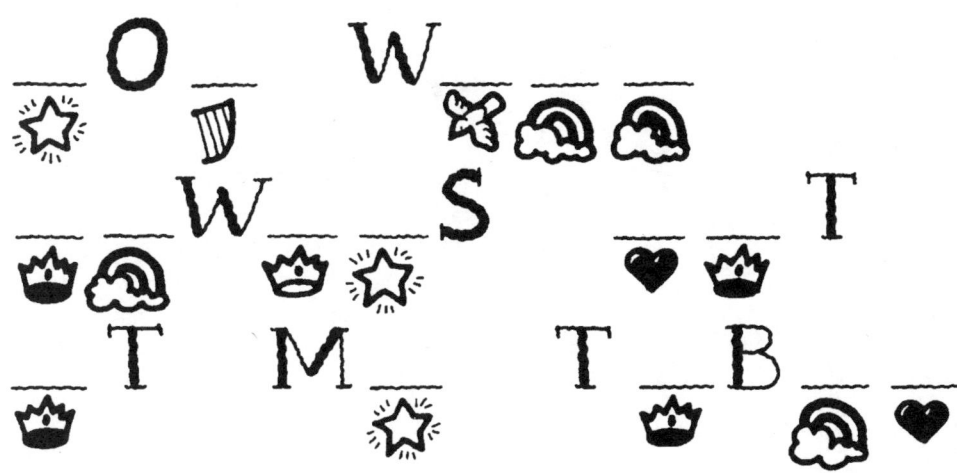

(2 Samuel 9:7)

29

Help David remember the events of his life. Unscramble the words to complete David's memories.
If you need help, look up the stories in your Bible.

1. _____ (Sualme) anointed me to be king.

[1 Samuel 16:13]

4. God gave me a gift for playing the _____ (ryle), I loved to write and sing _____ (lpassm).

[1 Samuel 16:16, 23; Psalm 23]

5. My best friend was _____ (onaJnhat).

[1 Samuel 18:1]

2. I was a _____ (heerspdh).

[1 Samuel 16:19]

3. My father's name was _____ (sseJe).

[1 Samuel 16:19]

6. I first became the king of _____ (dJuha) and later became the king of all _____ (rleIas).

[2 Samuel 2:4; 5:3]

7. I brought the _____ ___ ___ _____ (kar fo hte doLr) also called the ___ ___ ___ _____ (rak fo eht ocnveatn) to Jerusalem.

[2 Samuel 6:17; Exodus 25:22]

8. I returned all of Saul's land to his grandson _____ . (epMshhiobhte)

[2 Samuel 9:6-7]

9. I wanted to build a Temple in Jerusalem, but my son _____ (loSmnoo) will build the Temple.

[1 Kings 5:1-12]

30

DEBORAH and Barak sang a great song.
There was peace in the land forty years long.

Why had there been war in Deborah's land?

Judges 5:1, 8, 31

31

DEMETRIUS was very good.
He behaved as all of us should.

Who spoke well of Demetrius?

3 John 11-12

32

DORCAS was sick, then she died.
All her friends cried and cried.

What did Peter say to Dorcas?

Acts 9:39-40

33

ELIJAH and **ELISHA** were prophets
whose names are almost alike.
They always walked from place to place
since they didn't have
a plane or a car or a bike.

How did Elijah go to heaven?

2 Kings 2:11

34
ELIZABETH was very old,
Her husband, Zechariah, was very bold.

Who was the son of Elizabeth and
Zechariah?

_____

Luke 1:13

35
The gospel taught by **EPAPHRAS**
Was taught to people of every class.

Who was Epaphras?

_____

Colossians 1:5-7

36
ESTHER was a lovely young queen.
She knew Haman, who was grouchy and mean.

To whom did Esther tell the story of the evil Haman?

_____

Esther 7:1-6

Read Esther 2:2-23 if you need help completing the crossword puzzle.

Across

1. When I became queen, the king gave a great party called "Esther's _____" to celebrate. (Esther 2:18)
3. My husband's life was saved when Mordecai reported that he had overheard a plot to _____ King Ahasuerus. (Esther 2:21-23)
5. The person who raised me and helped to guide me in my life was _____. (Esther 2:7)
6. Mordecai advised me not to tell anyone at the palace that I was a _____. (Esther 2: 5, 10)
7. One of the king's servants named _____ helped me prepare to meet the king. (Esther 2:8-9)
8. Mordecai and I lived in the citadel of _____. (Esther 2:5)

Down

2. I became the queen when I married King _____. (Esther 2:16-17)
4. You know me as Esther, but my Jewish name is _____ (Esther 2:7)
5. My cousin _____ raised me after my parents died. (Esther 2:7)

Write a postcard message to a person who guides and helps you. Tell the person how much you appreciate the love and respect you receive.

38

EZEKIEL spoke some mighty words of God.
Even today, some folks thing they're odd.

Who was Ezekiel?

_____

Ezekiel 1:1-3

39

He must have thought his lunch was funny,
But when he ate it, it tasted like honey!

What did **EZEKIEL** eat?

_____

Ezekiel 3:1-4

40

FELIX and **FESTUS** had
talked about Paul.
They thought he was mad,
couldn't understand him at all.

What did Felix want Paul to give to him?

_____

Acts 24:25-26

41

What did **FESTUS** tell King Agrippa?

_____

Acts 25:13-14

42

The man who advised,
"Let these men go free,"
Was **GAMALIEL**,
the wisest Pharisee.

Did the council follow Gamaliel's advice?

Acts 5:34, 38-40

43

GEHAZI was very impolite
to the Shunammite
Who had said, "Everything's all right."

What did Gehazi do to the woman?

---

2 Kings 4:25-27

44

The Lord God said to **GIDEON**:
"You have too many men,
So I cannot give you
the camp of Midian.'

How many men did God finally let Gideon have?

Judges 7:15-16

45

GOMER was an unfaithful wife.
She was unfaithful almost all her life.

Who was Gomer's husband?

_____

Hosea 1:2-3

46

You must look, look, and look,
to find the book **HABAKKUK.**

Which two books of the Bible is Habakkuk between?

_____

47

HANNAH was Samuel's mother.
He had two sisters and three brothers.

What did Hannah tell her husband?

_____

1 Samuel 1:22

48

HERODIAS, a woman who was very cruel, thought John the Baptist was a fool.

What did Herodias tell her daughter to ask for?

_____

Mark 6:21-24

49

HEZEKIAH was one of Judah's best kings. He broke and smashed all kinds of bad things.

What did Hezekiah break and smash?

_____

2 Kings 18:1-4

50

There is quite a cost
If you choose to lose
What **HYMENAEUS** lost.

What did Hymenaeus lose?

_____

1 Timothy 1:18-20

51

ISAIAH told Ahaz of Judah,
"Be careful,
keep calm,
and don't be afraid.
The enemies of Judah
will not invade."

Who were some of the enemies Isaiah named?

Isaiah 7:4-7

52

We know very little about **ISCAH**.
She did have a sister named Milcah.

Who was her father?

Genesis 11:29

53

Judas **ISCARIOT**
betrayed Jesus.
We pray with God's help
it won't be said of us.

How many coins did the priests give Judas?

Matthew 26:14-16

Use your Bible to find the answers to the questions,
then find those words in the word search.

1. Rebekah's brother _ _ _ _ _ (Geneses 27:43)

2. Jacob's brother _ _ _ _ (Geneses 25:25)

3. What Jacob called the place of his dream _ _ _ _ _ _ (Geneses 28:19)

4. Leah's maidservent _ _ _ _ _ _ (Genesis 30:9)

5. Place where Laban lived. _ _ _ _ _ _ (Genesis 27:43)

6. Jacob's first wife _ _ _ _ (Genesis 29:25)

7. Former name of Bethel _ _ _ (Genesis 28:19)

8. Zilpah's first son _ _ _ (Genesis 30:9-11)

9. Leah's fourth son _ _ _ _ _ (Genesis 29:35)

10. The wife Jacob loved _ _ _ _ _ _ (Genesis 29:25)

11. Rachel's first son _ _ _ _ _ _ (Genesis 30:24)

12. Rachel's second son _ _ _ _ _ _ _ _ (Genesis 35:18)

N	R	A	C	H	E	L	W	I
I	Z	I	L	P	A	H	E	F
M	H	A	T	H	A	D	U	J
A	A	O	S	E	S	T	A	R
J	R	S	L	U	Z	F	I	G
N	A	E	N	E	E	S	A	U
E	N	A	D	N	A	B	A	L
B	O	Z	H	P	E	S	O	J
G	A	B	E	T	H	E	L	E

55

JEHOSHAPHAT, Jehoshaphat,
Was there really a king
With a name like that?

Was Jehoshaphat a good man?

_____

2 Chronicles 20:31-32

56

JEMIMAH's name means "little dove."
I bet she was full of peace and love.

Who was Jemimah's father?

_____

Job 42:12-14

57

His father was Hilkiah.
He prophesied to King Josiah,
Also to King Zedekiah.
His name was **JEREMIAH**.

Who promised to protect Jeremiah?

_____

Jeremiah 1:18-19

58

A covenant is a promise between two people or between God and God's people.

There are many covenants recorded in the Bible. Find each of the covenants listed here in your Bible. Who made each covenant?

Genesis 17:1-8
A covenant between _____ and _____

Genesis 21:25-32
A covenant between _____ and _____

Exodus 34:1-10
A covenant between _____ and _____

Genesis 31:43-46, 51-52
A covenant between _____ and _____

1 Chronicles 11:3
A covenant between _____ and _____

Exodus 19:5-6a
A covenant between _____ and _____

Genesis 9:8-17
A covenant between _____ and _____

Genesis 12:1-2
A covenant between _____ and _____

Psalm 132:11-12
A covenant between _____ and _____

Jeremiah spoke for God when he said that God would make a new covenant with the people. Read Jeremiah 31:31-34. Then write the new covenant from verse 33 here.

_____

_____

_____

_____

People have broken their covenants many times. But God's covenant has never been broken.

59

Wonderful Counselor
Mighty God
Everlasting Father
Prince of Peace
The Lord Is Our Righteousness
Samuel
Jonathan
Abigail
Mephibosheth
Jesus
Messiah
Savior
David
Solomon
Hannah

In Bible times names were chosen to say something about the persons being named. The Old Testament prophets Isaiah and Jeremiah tell some special names for the promised Messiah. We know that the Messiah was Jesus, our Savior. Search the puzzle to find these names for the Messiah and the names of some Old Testament persons. Names may be spelled from left to right, from top to bottom, or diagonally.

```
J E F F E V E R L A S T I N G F A T H E R
A N N E T T E J U A N H L A U R A R U T H
N B N D A N N I E L L E Y T R A C H E L A
E R A W O N D E R F U L C O U N S E L O R
D A N A A G D T L H S O L O M O N R I B O
O N C Y D I O H U S M R O S E R J I L R L
N D Y N E N M A K J A D A M G S A C A I D
A O J E L A I N E O E I S I S O S A S A A
L N O G L A N R R H V S H A N N O N H N N
D V A L E R I E R N E O M A R Y N J O N N
D K D M N N Q D I O N U P S H A R O N A Y
O E R E P O U E E E R O X A R M D D E B
U V I P E L E L M L I R E B M A R I A V O
G I E H G D E L I N L I I E T Y E I V A N
L N N I C O L E C M I G H T Y G O D I N N
A M Y B R A D E H M A H E H J Y M E D S I
S T P O O N O M E I M T A R E N A L I S E
D Y A S N F N E L L J E T O S A T I M T H
D L U H P E M L L O I O S A U L T Z B E E
A E L E A L O I E I M U N S S I H A R P A
R R A T T I L S C S O S F A I S E B I H T
R C L H T C L S H A N N A H T A W E D A H
E L A C Y I Y A E E A E L I H H H T G N E
L I N D A A N D R E A S M S A R A H E I R
L A U R I E L O R I N S A V I O R N T E D
```

CAN YOU ALSO FIND ANY FIRST NAMES OF PERSONS IN THE CLASS OR OF PERSONS YOU KNOW?

60

Use your Bible to discover who said each statement. Draw a line to match the words with the correct picture. (Caution: You may need to read a few verses before or after each clue to find the answer. And note: only five are direct quotes. The other three are what we know people said from what the story tells us.)

Where is the child who has been born king of the Jews? (Matthew 2:2)

Do not be afraid, for see — I am bringing you good news of great joy for all the people: to you is born this day in the city of David a Savior, who is the Messiah, the Lord. (Luke 2:10-11)

I have no room for you, but you may sleep in my stable where the animals are kept. (Luke 2:7)

My eyes have seen your salvation. (Luke 2:30)

Let us go now to Bethlehem and see this thing that has taken place, which the Lord has made known to us. (Luke 2:15)

I will take Mary as my wife. We shall name the child she will bear Jesus. (Matthew 1:20-21)

Here am I, the servant of the Lord; let it be with me according to your word. (Luke 1:38)

I am an old woman. I have waited many years for this child who will bring redemption to Jerusalem. (Luke 2:38)

Innkeeper

Simeon

Shepherds

Angel

Mary

Wise Men

Anna

Joseph

61

Use your Bible to find twelve people who wanted to see Jesus.
Then find those same people in the word search.

1. Luke 2:15-17 _ _ _ _ _ _ _ _ _

2. Luke 2:27 _ _ _ _ _ _

3. Luke 2:36-38 _ _ _ _

4. Matthew 2:1 _ _ _ _   _ _ _

5. Matthew 3 _ _ _ _   _ _ _   _ _ _ _ _ _ _

6. Matthew 8:1-3 _ _ _ _ _

7. Matthew 15:22 _ _ _ _ _ _ _ _ _ _   _ _ _ _ _

8. Mark 7:26 _ _ _ _ _ _ _ _ _ _ _ _ _ _ _   _ _ _ _ _

9. Mark 10:46 _ _ _ _ _ _ _ _ _

10. Luke 7:1-10 _ _ _ _ _ _ _ _ _

11. Luke 7:1-15 _ _ _ _ _ _

12. John 3:1 _ _ _ _ _ _ _ _ _

```
W I S E M E N H E A R T A T R E E A A
A C T O C E N T U R I O N E O X C B N
T E M N I C O D E M U S P S T A R A N
C C E N G L I S H S H E P H E R D S A
H H O J J A M E S O L S I M E O N R S
S Y R O P H O E N I C I A N W O M A N
W I W H B A R T I M A E U S A F P U T
B I C N T H E B A P T I S T V W A F G
D F D N O X T H E N I J O S E P H H H
K L M O Y N A M O W E T I N A A N A C
S A M M W C L E A N S O N G C H I L D
```

62
Let us
Let **JESUS**
Keep us.

Where should we keep ourselves?

_____

Jude, verse 21

63

JOANNA traveled with Jesus and his friends,
And often their clothes she would mend.

Besides Joanna, who else traveled with Jesus?

_____

_____

Luke 8:1-3

64

JOASH and **JOSIAH**
were not very old
When they became kings
they had to be bold.

How old was Joash when he became king of Judah?

_____

2 Chronicles 24:1

How old was Josiah when he became king of Judah?

_____

2 Kings 22:1

65

Before all his troubles
JOB had livestock in numbers.

How many livestock did he have at the end of his life?

_____

Job 42:12

66

JOHN ate locusts and wild honey.
He didn't have much use for money.

What kind of clothes did John wear?

_____

Mark 1:6

Jonah got more adventure than he planned! Instead of obeying God, Jonah tried to run and hide. Read Jonah 1:1-17; 2:1-2, 9-10; 3:1-3a in your Bible. Then answer the questions in your own words to review what happened to Jonah.

God called Jonah to go to Nineveh and _____

_____.

Instead, Jonah tried to escape God by going to _____.

On the way, what happened to threaten the safety of Jonah and the crew of the boat he traveled on?

_____

Instead of reaching his destination, Jonah was thrown

overboard and then _____

_____.

Inside the fish, Jonah had time to think. What was his prayer? (See Jonah 2:2a.)

_____

_____

Ultimately, Jonah ended up going to _____.

Trace Jonah's travels on the map. Decide where you think he was thrown into the sea. The **X** shows where Jonah was spit out on dry land.

If you were a travel agent planning Jonah's travels, what would have been his destination and why? How would he have gotten there?

68

Recall the story of Jonah in Nineveh. Read it again in Jonah 3:1 — 4:11 if you need help.

The Lord came to — $\underline{20}$ $\underline{30}$ — — — a second time and said, "Go to — $\underline{15}$ — $\underline{37}$ $\underline{7}$ — ." Jonah obeyed God.
In Nineveh he said, " In $\underline{3}$ — $\underline{5}$ $\underline{16}$ — days the city will be destroyed!" The people believed Jonah.
They $\underline{18}$ $\underline{6}$ — — $\underline{22}$ $\underline{29}$ and put on — $\underline{33}$ — — — — $\underline{34}$ $\underline{1}$ $\underline{9}$ to say that they were sorry and that they would change.
The King said, "Who knows? God may — — — — $\underline{26}$ — — $\underline{42}$ — — us and we will not $\underline{27}$ $\underline{10}$ $\underline{28}$ $\underline{11}$ — — .
Jonah was — $\underline{12}$ — $\underline{21}$ $\underline{19}$ and said to God, "See! I knew you were a — — — — — $\underline{13}$ $\underline{4}$ $\underline{14}$ — God." Jonah went out of the — $\underline{38}$ $\underline{35}$ $\underline{25}$ and sat down.
God made a — — $\underline{41}$ — grow that pleased Jonah. The next day, however, a worm attacked the bush and Jonah had no shade. — $\underline{17}$ $\underline{32}$ knew that Jonah was mad and said," You are concerned about the — — — $\underline{2}$ — $\underline{36}$. I am concerned for the $\underline{23}$ $\underline{8}$ — — — $\underline{24}$ $\underline{31}$ in Nineveh."

Now transfer each numbered letter to the correct numbered space to find a Bible verse that explains God's actions in Nineveh.

Y $\underline{1}$ $\underline{2}$ — $\underline{3}$ $\underline{4}$ $\underline{5}$ G $\underline{6}$ $\underline{7}$ $\underline{8}$ — $\underline{9}$ H $\underline{10}$

— $\underline{11}$ $\underline{12}$ $\underline{13}$ Q $\underline{14}$ $\underline{15}$ Y $\underline{16}$ — $\underline{17}$ $\underline{18}$ — $\underline{19}$ $\underline{20}$ U $\underline{21}$

P $\underline{22}$ O $\underline{23}$ $\underline{24}$ E;

$\underline{25}$ $\underline{26}$ U $\underline{27}$ A $\underline{28}$ $\underline{29}$ O $\underline{30}$ $\underline{31}$ $\underline{32}$ — $\underline{33}$ L $\underline{34}$

$\underline{35}$ $\underline{36}$ $\underline{37}$ $\underline{38}$ R $\underline{41}$ $\underline{42}$ N.

Psalm 85:2

69

KADMIEL and all his friends
Told the people,
"Praise the Lord your God,"
And hoped they wouldn't just pretend.

What did he and his friends say about God?

_____

Nehemiah 9:5

70

KETURAH married a man named Abraham.
Three of their sons
Were Zimran, Jokshan, and Medan.

Who were Keturah's other three sons?

_____

Genesis 25:1-2

71

KEZIAH and Keren-Happuch
Were two more daughters
Job loved very much.

What did Keziah look like?

_____

Job 42:14-15

72

LEAH had six sons and a daughter.
Jacob was their famous father.

What was Leah's daughter named?

_____

Genesis 30:20-21

73

LEMUEL wrote Proverbs
chapter thirty-one.
He was a faithful,
obedient son.
He wrote about a wife
who couldn't be outdone.

Who taught Lemuel his lessons?

_____

Proverbs 31:1

74

LOIS was Timothy's grandmother.
We don't know his grandfather.

Who was Lois' daughter?

_____

2 Timothy 1:5

75

The last word in **MALACHI's** book
is "curse."
He stopped right there
so it wouldn't be worse.

What did Malachi say would happen to the fathers
and the children?

_____

Malachi 4:6

76

Hezekiah told Isaiah,
"The Lord's words are good"
His son **MANASSEH**
Never did the things he should.

What did Manasseh do?

_____

_____

2 Kings 21:2-6

77

MARTHA was a very hard worker.
Often Jesus came to visit her.

What did Martha do when she heard
Jesus was coming?

_____

_____

John 11:20

78

When the angel told Mary that she would be the mother of Jesus, she was surprised. Decode the puzzle to discover Mary's response to God.

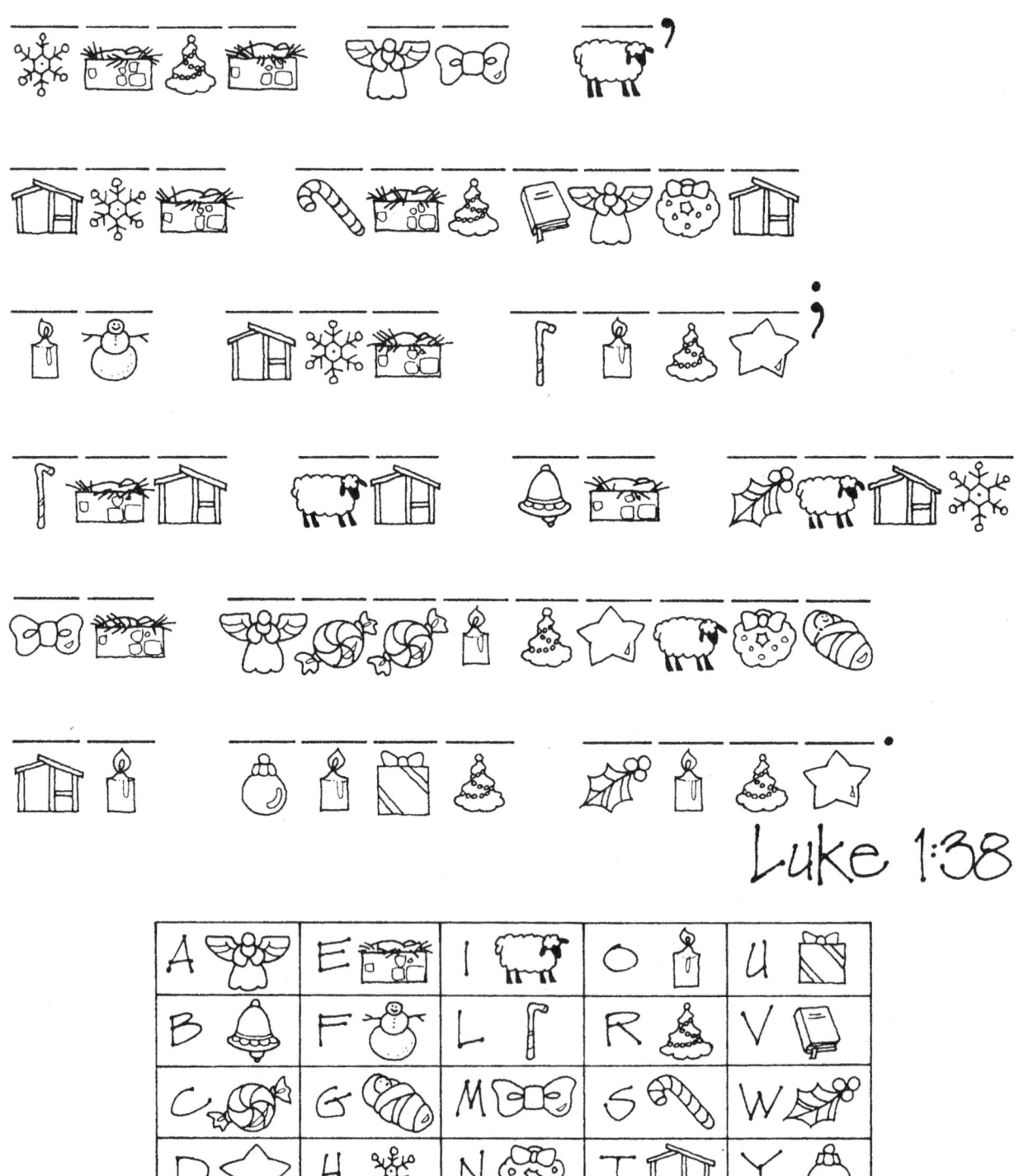

Luke 1:38

79

MELCHIZEDEK was priest forever.
Forever never ends,
Never, never, never.

What did Abraham give Melchizedek?

_____

Hebrews 7:1-2, 17

80

MIRIAM had two famous brothers.
Aaron was one, Moses the other.

What did Miriam and the women do once the
Israelites were safe?

_____

Exodus 15:20

81

MOSES led the people out of slavery.
This is true and honest history.

Who were the other two people with Moses?

_____

Micah 6:4

82

NAHUM's book is number thirty-four.
After it there are only five more.

What city does Nahum talk about?

_____

Nahum 1:1

83

David did lament,
"Nathan, I am not content.
I must repent.
I live in a palace,
While God's ark is in a tent."

What did **NATHAN** tell David to do?

_____

1 Chronicles 17:1-2

84
A Wall Is Built

"Why are you so sad?" asked his cupbearer.  breathed a prayer to God before he answered.

"  is in ruins. There is no  around the city. I would like to go to  to help."

"Go," said the  "When got to 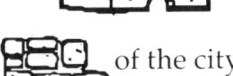, he rode around the old  of the city. Mounds and heaps and piles of bricks and dirt were everywhere! Even the gates had been burned.

 said, "Anyone can enter our city to harm us! But God has put it into my heart to rebuild the  ."

Each family agreed to do one part of the . They worked cheerfully because they knew that God was helping them.

At last the  was done!  arranged a great celebration to praise God. Some of the people carried  to make music. Special groups of singers learned songs of thanksgiving to sing to God.  asked the people to march in two groups and meet at the  to give thanks to God. It was like a great parade! Everyone shouted and sang and prayed. The joy of Jerusalem was heard far away.

Based on Nehemiah 2:2-6, 11-18; 12:27-43

King Artaxerxes

Nehemiah

Jerusalem

wall

harps, cymbals, and lyres

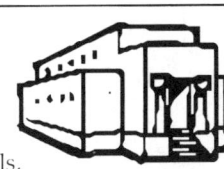
Temple

Across

2. Sold purple cloth (Acts 16:14)
3. A tax collector (Matthew 9:9)
7. Brother of James (Matthew 4:21)
9. Welcomed Jesus into her home (Luke 10:38)
11. Wept at Jesus' tomb (John 20:1, 11)
14. Betrayed Jesus with kiss (Mark 14:43-46)
16. Called a Zealot (Luke 6:15)
17. Denied Jesus three times (Mark 14:72)
18. His Hebrew name was Saul (Acts 26:1, 14)
20. Provided for Jesus (Luke 8:3)
21. Heard about Jesus from Philip (John 1:45)
22. Provided for Jesus (Luke 8:3)

Down

1. Wife of Aquila; tentmaker (Acts 18:2-3)
4. Was called "the Twin" (John 20:24)
5. Mother of Jesus (Luke 1:30-31)
6. Maid who welcomed Peter (Acts 12:13-14)
7. Brother of John, son of Zebedee (Mark 1:19)
8. Another name for the disciple called Nathanael in John 1:47, begins with the letter *B* (Matthew 10:3)
10. Another Judas. He was often called by a name that begins with the letter *T*. (Matthew 10:3)
12. Simon Peter's brother (John 1:40-41)
13. Made clothes (Acts 9:39)
15. One of the women who went to anoint Jesus' body (Mark 16:1)
17. Said to Jesus, "Show us the Father." (John 14:8)
19. A missionary with Paul (Acts 13:2-4)

What can you remember about each of the persons, places, and important words hidden in this word search? As you find each word, think about how it is related to the story of Paul's missionary trips.

```
I J E R U S A L E M K T E N T M A K E R E B R
J C E L A I O P H I L I P P I E W Q R L I E N
H U O S I Q S Y R I A M A O T G N P P K J R O
E I O R U O U W E R T O P E R G A R O O K O F
A U P R I S C I L L A T H I S U U N I O E E I
C C N I C N * O L O H H O K L P E C T R O A S
I L A I H H T C O A I Y S O Y O E K N I E W H
N H O E C O R H H I Y E S F S I I C T C O I G
O B T O S E O I N R I U Y P T O K S O O C C J
L E A I I A M I S S I O N A R Y O A A N E I H
A G O R A I R I Z T O S I K A O H J K I I K N
S A S A N F M E L F I L T D E R B E I U D I O
S R A I O A U U A I P A R T N E R W I M I Y Q
E U L N L I B I E R G E N T I L E S O P U K L
H O I A I B H A T H E N S S O H S U S E H P E
T C S I U N B G S U S R A T A I N O D E C A M
```

People
Aquila
Barnabas
Eunice
Jesus Christ
Lois
Lydia
Paul
Priscilla
Silas
Timothy

Places
Antioch
Athens
Beroea
Caesarea
Corinth
Derbe
Ephesus
Iconium
Jerusalem
Lystra
Macedonia
Paphos
Perga
Philippi
Salamis
Syria
Tarsus
Thessalonica
Troas

Other Important Words
Christians
Courage
Faith
Fish
Gentiles
Jews
Missionary
Purple
Tentmaker
Partner
Rejoice

87
NICODEMUS went to
Jesus one night.
He wanted to learn
everything right.

How did Jesus answer the question Nicodemus asked?

_____

John 3:4-8

88
The book of **OBADIAH**
has only chapter one.
The book of Obadiah
has verses twenty-one.

Whose kingdom will be in the mountains,
according to Obadiah?

_____

Obadiah, verse 21

89
OG was a king
Who was tall and fat.
He was a giant—
Just think about that.

How big was Og's bed?

_____

Deuteronomy 3:11

90

ONESIMUS was sent back home.
He did not want to be in Rome.

Who sent Onesimus home?

_____

Philemon, verses 9-12

91

ORPHA decided to say at her mother's home.
She did not leave with Naomi to roam.

What did Orpha do when Naomi left?

_____

Ruth 1:14

Use your Bible to complete the crossword puzzle. You can find the names and places in the stories in Acts 11:19-26 and Acts 13:1-5, 14. Read carefully!

Across

3. Barnabas went to this city to find Paul and bring him to Antioch.
5. The followers of Jesus were scattered because of the persecution that resulted in the stoning of this man.
6. Paul and Barnabas went to this city in Cyprus after leaving Seleucia.
7. The Antioch where Paul and Barnabas started the first group called Christians was in Syria. The other Antioch was in this region.

8. The place where believers in Christ were first called Christians was in this city in Syria.

Down

1. When the Jerusalem church heard about the group of believers in Antioch, they sent this man to find out what was happening there.
2. When the Christians scattered from Jerusalem, some men who were from Cyprus and Cyrene came to this city in Syria.
4. In Antioch the believers were first called by this name that is still used today.

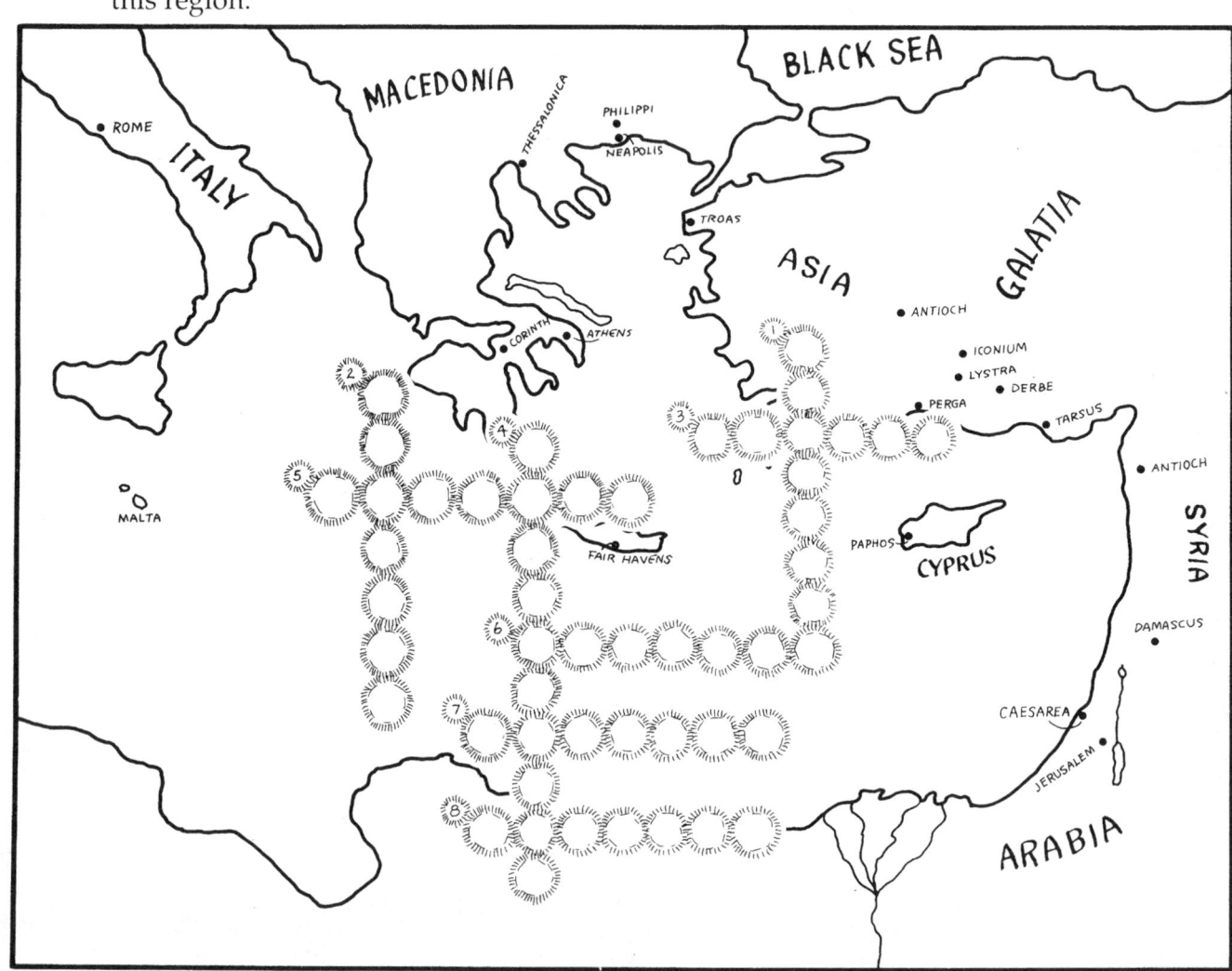

93
Discover Paul's Secret

Even when he was in prison, Paul wrote to the churches he had started. Read part of one of Paul's letters in Philippians 1:12-14. You will discover that even in prison, Paul trusted God.

Then read Philippians 4:11-13 to help you fill in the missing words from one of Paul's letters. Write one letter per box or circle.

I have learned to be ☐○☐☐☐☐☐ with whatever

I have. I know what it is to have ☐☐☐☐☐○ , and I

know what it is to have plenty. In any and all

○☐☐☐☐☐☐☐☐☐☐☐☐ I

have learned the ☐☐☐○☐☐ of being well-fed and

of going ☐○☐☐☐☐ , of having plenty and of being

in need. I can do ○☐☐ things through him who

☐☐☐☐☐○☐☐☐☐ me.

Philippians 4:11-13

Now write the letters with circles around them in the circles below

○○○○○○

Unscramble the letters in the circles to make a word.
Use a separate piece of paper if you need to.
Write the word in the sentence below.

Paul's faith gave him _____ and helped him to trust God.

Now read the sentence to learn Paul's secret.

94

Multiply Forgiveness

Peter came to Jesus and asked, "Lord, if another member of the church sins against me, how often should I forgive? As many as seven times?" (Matthew 18:21)

Discover Jesus' response by cracking the code in the multiplication table. Multiply the numbers and assign the corresponding letters to the blanks in the code.

B
$6 \times 6 =$ ____

L
$9 \times 6 =$ ____

O
$7 \times 7 =$ ____

U
$3 \times 1 =$ ____

E
$4 \times 3 =$ ____

M
$7 \times 2 =$ ____

S
$3 \times 5 =$ ____

V
$9 \times 9 =$ ____

I
$5 \times 8 =$ ____

N
$8 \times 3 =$ ____

T
$10 \times 8 =$ ____

Y
$7 \times 4 =$ ____

"___ ___ ___ ___ ___ ___ ___ ___ ___ ___ ___ ___ ___,'
24 49 80 15 12 81 12 24 80 40 14 12 15

___ ___ ___,' ___ ___ ___ ___ ___ ___ ___ ___ ___,'
36 3 80   40   80 12 54 54   28 49 3

___ ___ ___ ___ ___ ___ ___ - ___ ___ ___ ___ ___ ___
15 12 81 12 24 80 28   15 12 81 12 24

___ ___ ___ ___ ___." (Matthew 18:22)
80 40 14 12 15

A footnote in your Bible tells you that Jesus' answer may also be translated "seventy times seven." How many times would that be?

_____

Whether Jesus said 77 times or 490 times, what do you suppose Jesus meant? _____

_____

Is there a limit to God's forgiveness? _____

95

PETHUEL was father of a prophet.
We know about him just this little bit,
And so his name we won't omit.

Who was Pethuel's son?

_____

Joel 1:1

96

The wife was **PRISCILLA.**
The husband was Aquila.

What group of people met at the home of
Aquila and Priscilla?

_____

1 Corinthians 16:19

Do you remember the messages delivered by the people who spoke for God during Old Testament times? Check your memory by reading the clues and completing the crossword puzzle.

If you need help, find the stories in your Bible.

ACROSS

2. Traveled to Jerusalem to help the people rebuild the city walls. (Nehemiah 2:4-5)

5. Interpreted the meaning of a scroll found in the Temple by King Josiah's workmen. (2 Kings 22:14-16)

7. Showed that there is only one God by praying to God in a contest on Mount Carmel. (1 Kings 18:30-39)

10. The king who ordered the cleanup of the Temple, where the Book of the Law was found. (2 Kings 22:3-6)

11. Climbed a high wooden platform and read God's law aloud. (Nehemiah 8:1-4a)

12. Described God's law as a plumb line that we can use to measure our lives. (Amos 7:7-8)

13. Called for peace. (Micah 4:1-5)

14. Spoke of a day when war would end and people would "beat their swords into plowshares." (Micah 4:3-4)

DOWN

1. Told the people that "The Lord requires that you do justice, love kindness, and walk humbly with your God." (Micah 6:8)

3. Was a female prophet. (2 Kings 22:11-14)

4. Called to be a prophet when he was still a youth. (Jeremiah 1:1, 4-7)

6. Called for justice. (Amos 5:24)

8. Called for love and forgiveness by loving and forgiving his wife who had run away. (Hosea 1:1)

9. Continued to speak God's word even when the scroll he had written was cut into pieces and burned, and even when he was thrown into a deep, muddy well. (Jeremiah 36:27-28, 32; 38:6, 10-13, 17)

Find the names of the prophets and the issues they preached about. Cross the words off as you find them in the puzzle.

Jeremiah — Obey
Amos — Justice
Hosea — Love
Micah — Peace
Elijah — Lord
Huldah — Amends

Words may go up, down, sideways, or diagonally.

O	B	J	Z	A	E	Y	M	H	X
E	U	N	E	E	L	I	J	A	H
V	W	F	C	R	C	E	U	D	M
O	J	A	O	A	E	Q	S	L	K
L	E	L	H	M	X	M	T	U	R
P	S	O	B	E	Y	S	I	H	N
J	W	R	U	N	V	O	C	A	T
A	L	D	P	D	S	M	E	M	H
M	Y	H	O	S	E	A	A	O	M

99
PUAH didn't obey the king.
For him she wouldn't do a thing.

What did Puah tell the king?

___

Exodus 1:15-19

100
In the home of Gaius
there was a meeting.
From our brother **QUARTUS**
comes a greeting.

What did Quartus' friend Erastus do?

___

Romans 16:23

101
Caesar Augustus
ordered a census.
Governor **QUIRINIUS**
knew he was serious.

Where was Quirinius governor?

___

Luke 2:1-3

102

Jacob loved **RACHEL**, not Leah,
Not Leah, Maria, or Dorothea.

What were Rachel and Leah like?

_____

_____

Genesis 29:16-18

103

REHOBOAM was the son
of a very wise father.
But as for taking good advice,
he wouldn't even bother.

Who was Rehoboam's father?

_____

2 Chronicles 10:6-8

104

REUBEN's brother Joseph
was a dreamer.
And his brother Judah
was a schemer.

What did Reuben suggest they do to Joseph?

_____

Genesis 37:17-24

105

RHODA was so happy and sunny;
She did something really funny.

What did Rhoda do?

_____

Acts 12:13-14

106

When **SAMUEL** died,
All Israel cried.

Where was Samuel buried?

_____

1 Samuel 25:1

107

SAPPHIRA lied,
Then she died.

What did Peter ask Sapphira?

_____

Acts 5:1-2, 8

108

SARAH made her very best bread.
She made it from a recipe
She kept in her head.

Who told Sarah to make the bread?

_____

Genesis 18:6

109

SILAS,* Timothy, and Paul
Wrote words of great encouragement.
Now we can read them all
In the books we call the New Testament.

What do Silas, Timothy, and Paul have that is growing?

_____

2 Thessalonians 1:1-4

*NOTE: "Silas" is "Silvanus" in some Bible versions.

Read Luke 2:22-38. Then unscramble the words in the candy jar. Write the correct word in each blank to complete the story.

_____ had been waiting many years for

God to keep the promise to allow him to see the

Lord's _____. One day Simeon was guided

by the _____ to go to the _____.

At the Temple Simeon saw _____ and

_____ who had brought their baby

son _____ to be presented to the Lord.

When Simeon saw the child, he held the baby

and _____ God. Simeon said to God,

"My eyes have seen your _____."

When the prophet _____ saw Jesus, she too

began to _____ God.

What does the birth of Jesus mean to you today?

_____

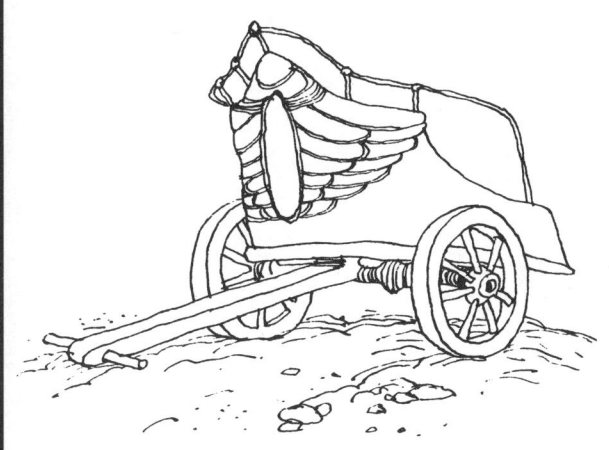

111

King **SOLOMON**
made a fancy carriage
To take him about
on the day of his marriage.

What color was the seat in Solomon's
carriage?

_____

Song of Solomon 3:9-10

112

TAMAR was a beautiful woman.
Her father's name was Absalom.

How many brothers did Tamar have?

_____

2 Samuel 14:27

113

TERAH moved away from home.
For a while he had to roam.

Who was Terah's son?

_____

Genesis 11:31

114

TIMOTHY was a good news reporter.
That's what he was—
Not a gossip supporter.

What was the good news Timothy gave to Paul
from the Thessalonians?

_____

1 Thessalonians 3:6

115

Paul looked and looked all around town,
But brother **TITUS** could not be found.

Was Paul upset about Titus?

_____

2 Corinthians 2:12-13

116

TRYPHENA lived in Rome—
That city was her home.

What was Tryphena's sister named?

_____

Romans 16:12

117

"Yes, I'm serious,"
fusses old **URBANUS**,
"Names that end is 'us'
are much too numerous."

What did Urbanus do?

_____

Romans 16:9

118

URIAH was strong and brave—a Hittite.
He slept by the palace gate one night.

Who was with Uriah?

_____

2 Samuel 11:9

119

When **UZZIAH** was king
The earth did shake.
When Uzziah was king
The earth did quake.

In what country was Uzziah king?

_____

Zechariah 14:5

120

Only once each can we find these names:
VANIAH,
Bedeiah,
and Mattaniah.
They are not in the books by:
Nehemiah,
Jeremiah,
or Obadiah.

What had Vaniah and his brothers done?

Ezra 10:35-37, 44

121

The king ordered Queen **VASHTI**
To come before him at his party.
When she told him no,
He thought she was a smarty.

How did the king behave when Vashti said no?

Esther 1:11-12, 19

122

VOPHSI'S son Nahbi
Was sent to scout the land,
To see if the land
Really was grand.

What tribe were Vophsi and Nahbi from?

_____

Numbers 13:14, 16, 30-33

123

The **WIDOW** gave all she had,
"It's more than enough, " Jesus said.

How much did the widow put in the collection?

_____

Luke 21:1-4

124

On entering the house, they saw the child with Mary his
mother; and they knelt down and paid him homage. Then,
opening their treasure chests, they offered him gifts of gold,
frankincense, and myrrh. (Matthew 2:11)

Read about these gifts in your Bible.

Gold was probably the first metal known to human beings. It is mentioned many times in the Bible as a metal of great value.

Exodus 25:17
The mercy seat (cover) of the ark of the covenant (in which the stone tablets of the Ten Commandments were kept) was made of _____ _____.

Exodus 35:22
When the Tabernacle was built in the wilderness, the people brought many gold objects as an _____ to the Lord.

1 Peter 1:7
Although gold is very valuable, the genuineness of your _____ is more precious than gold.

Luke 6:31
This familiar verse is known as the _____ _____ because of its great value.

Myrrh was a fragrant resin valued by people in Bible times for its many uses.

Exodus 30:23-25
Myrrh was one of the important ingredients used to make a sacred _____ _____.

Mark 15:23
At his crucifixion Jesus was offered a mixture of _____ and _____ to relieve his pain. However, Jesus did not take it.

John 19:39-40
Jesus' body was wrapped in linen cloths and a mixture of spices including _____ and _____.

Frankincense was a fragrant gum resin used in making incense to be burned as an offering to God.

Exodus 30:34-36
List the ingredients of the holy incense that God told Moses to make.

_____

_____

_____

Exodus 30:37
The incense was not to be used for personal purposes but was to be regarded as _____ to the _____.

Leviticus 24:5-8
Frankincense was used in the Tabernacle as an offering. When Aaron placed the frankincense with the bread in the Tabernacle, it was a symbol of the commitment of the Israelite people. It was a sign of a _____ forever.

125

We don't know her name,
But her story is often told.
The **WOMAN AT THE WELL** was really quiet bold.

What did Jesus say he would give her?

_____

John 4:13-14

126

King **XERXES** ruled lands
from the west to the east.
He planned a banquet—
a very splendid feast,
Many people came—
the greatest to the least.

How many days did King Xerxes' banquet last?

_____

Esther 1:2-5

127

Euodia and Syntyche disagreed,
Paul asked his "true **YOKEFELLOW**" to intercede.

What did Paul say we should always do?

_____

Philippians 4:2-7

128

ZECHARIAH was very old.
When he spoke to Gabriel,
He was much too bold.

What happened to Zechariah?

_____

Luke 1:18-20

129

ZEPHANIAH has three chapters
In his little book.
It is a book
For which we really have to look.

Who was the king when Zephaniah spoke?

_____

Zephaniah 1:1

130

ZERUBBABEL, Zerubbabel,
It is a name I like to spell.
Z-E-R-U-B-B-A-B-E-L!

What did the Lord tell Zerubbabel?

_____

Haggai 2:4

131

ZIPPORAH was the woman Moses married.
When Moses went back to Egypt,
She packed up the children and all she could carry.

How did Zipporah meet Moses?

_____

Exodus 2:16-21

1
Moses

2
Nabal

3
bound his hands

4
Naboth

5

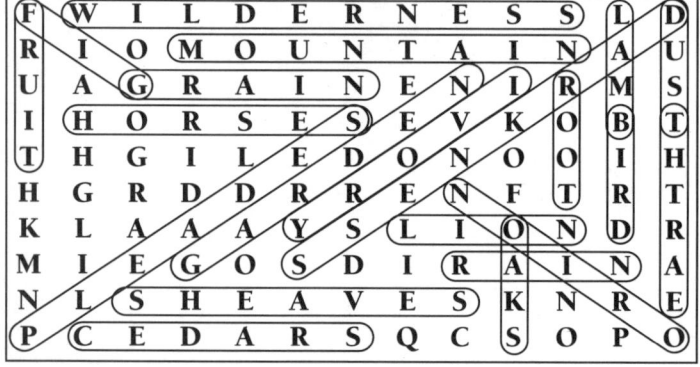

6
84

7
Zenas

8
turned off the road,
scraped against the wall,
lay down, and spoke

9
in response to a revelation

10
David

11
wrote on the wall
Daniel

12
Agrippa

13
Genesis 21:1-3
Abraham   Sarah
Isaac

Exodus 2:1-10; Numbers 26:59
Amram   Jochebed
Aaron   Miriam Moses

2 Timothy 1:1-2,5
Eunice   Lois
Timothy

Genesis 25:19-21,24-26
Isaac   Rebekah
Jacob   Esau

Luke 1:57-60
Zechariah   Elizabeth
John

14
1. Jonathan
2. David
3. Abraham
4. Eliphaz
5. Bildad
6. Zophar
7. Lazarus
8. Mary
9. Martha

✷ ANSWERS ✷

15
Abram
Samuel
Bezalel
Moses
Levi
Saul

16
Across
2. Apostles
4. Hezekiah
5. Jonah
7. Jesus
9. Israelites

Down
1. Stephen
3. Gideon
6. Hannah
8. Moses

17
Column 1
Tabitha
Dorcas
Priscilla
Miriam
Huldah

Column 2
Euodia, Syntyche
Deborah
Lydia
Phoebe

18
Boaz
Naomi
rich
farmer
glean
Naomi
reward, deeds
food
handfulls
Blessed

19
85

20
Eubulus, Pudens, Linus

21
Euodia, Syntyche

22
Zur

23
One

24
Nebuchadnezzar

25
knowledge
skill
literature
wisdom
insight

26

Judah
Hebron
Israel
Jerusalem
7 years and 6 months
33

27

Across
1. Jerusalem
5. Saul
7. Bethlehem
8. God
9. Lyre

Down
1. Jonathan
2. Abigail
3. Mephibosheth
4. Judah
6. Jesse

28

I WILL NEVER CUT OFF MY LOVE FROM
YOUR FAMILY

YOU WILL ALWAYS EAT AT MY TABLE

29

1. Samuel
2. Shepherd
3. Jesse
4. lyre
5. psalms
6. Jonathan
7. Judah, Israel
8. Ark of the Lord,
   Ark of the Covenant
9. Mephibosheth
10. Solomon

30

the people worshiped other gods

31

everyone

32

"Get up"

33

chariot of fire

34

John

35

a fellow worker of Paul

36

King Xerxes (Ahasuerus)

37

Across
1. banquet
3. assassinate
5. Mordecai
6. Jew
7. Hegai
8. Susa

Down
2. Ahasuerus
4. Hadassah
5. Mordecai

38

a priest

39

a scroll

40

money (a bribe)

41

Paul had been left in prison by Felix

42

yes

43

tried to push her away

44

300

45

Hosea

46

Nahum and Zephaniah

47

she would give Samuel to God

48

the head of John the Baptist

49

sacred stones and the bronze snake

50

faith

51

Aram, Ephraim, and Rezin

52

Haran

53

30

54

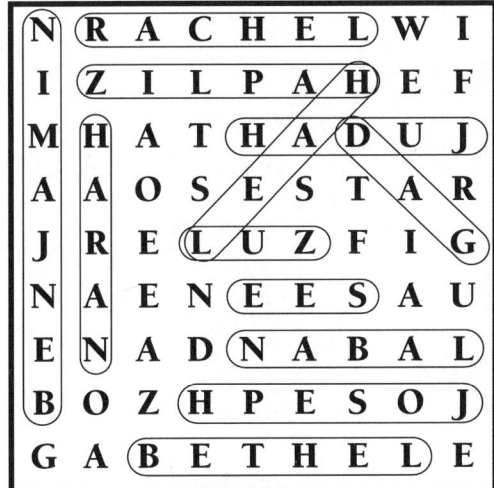

55

yes

56

Job

57

the Lord

58

Abram and God
Abraham and Abimelech
God and the Israelites
Laban and Jacob
David and the elders
God and the Israelites
God and Noah
God and Abram
God and David

59

```
J E F F E V E R L A S T I N G F A T H E R
A N N E T T E J U A N H L A U R A R U T H
N B N D A N N I E L L E Y T R A C H E L A
E R A W O N D E R F U L C O U N S E L O R
D A N A A G D T L H S O L O M O N R I B O
O N C Y D I O H U S M R O S E R J I L R L
N D Y N E N M A K J A D A M G S A C A I D
A O J E L A I N E O E I S O S A S A A D
L N O G L A N R R H V S H A N N O N H N N
D V A L E R I E R N E O M A R Y N J O N Y
D K D M N N Q D I O N U P S H A R O N A Y
O E R E P O U E E E R O X A R M D D E B O
U V I P E L E L M L I R E B M A R I A V N
G I E H G D E L I N I E T Y E I V A N
L N N I C O L E M I G H T Y G O D I N N
A M Y B R A D E H M A H E H J Y M E D S
S T P O O N O M E I M T A R E N A L I S E
D Y A S N F N E L L J E T O S A T I M T H
D L U H P E M L L O I O S A U L T Z B E E
A E L E A L O I E I M U N S S I H A R P A
R R A T I L S C S O S F A I S E B I H T
R C L H T C L S H A N N A H T A W E D A H
E L A C Y I Y A E E A E L I H H H T G N E
L I N D A A N D R E A S M S A R A H E I R
L A U R I E L O R I N S A V I O R N T E D
```

61

```
W I S E M E N H E A R T A T R E E A A
A C T O C E N T U R I O N F O X C B N N
T E M N I C O D E M U S P S T A R A A
C C E N G L I S H S H E P H E R D S N
S Y R O P H O E N I C I A N W O M A N
W I W H B A R T I M A E U S A F P U T
B I C N T H E B A P T I S T V W A F G
D F D N O X T H E N I J O S E P H H
K L M O Y N A M O W E T I N A A N A C
S A M M W C L E A N S O N G C H I L D
```

62
in the love of God

63
Mary Magdalene
Susanna

64
seven
eight

65
14,000 sheep; 6,000 camels; 1,000 yoke of oxen; 1,000 donkeys

66
camel's hair

67
tell the people to repent
Tarshish
a storm came up
swallowed by a fish
he called to the Lord
Nineveh

60

Where is the child who has been born king of the Jews? (Matthew 2:2)

Do not be afraid, for see — I am bringing you good news of great joy for all the people: to you is born this day in the city of David a Savior, who is the Messiah, the Lord. (Luke 2:10-11)

I have no room for you, but you may sleep in my stable where the animals are kept. (Luke 2:7)

My eyes have seen your salvation. (Luke 2:30)

Let us go now to Bethlehem and see this thing that has taken place, which the Lord has made known to us. (Luke 2:15)

I will take Mary as my wife. We shall name the child she will bear Jesus. (Matthew 1:20-21)

Here am I, the servant of the Lord; let it be with me according to your word. (Luke 1:38)

I am an old woman. I have waited many years for this child who will bring redemption to Jerusalem. (Luke 2:38)

68

Jonah
Nineveh
forty
fasted
sackcloth
forgive
perish
angry
gracious
city
bush
God
bush
people

You forgave the iniquity of your people;
you pardoned all their sin.

69

Blessed be your glorious name

70

Midian, Ishbak, Shuah

71

she was beautiful

72

Dinah

73

his mother

74

Eunice

75

they would love each other

76

built altars and worshiped idols
practiced magic

77

she went to meet him

78

Here am I, the servant of
the Lord; let it be with me according to your
word.

79

one tenth of everything

80

sang and danced

81

Aaron and Miriam

82

Nineveh

83

Do all that you have in mind.

84

[no answers]

85

Across
2. Lydia
3. Matthew
7. John
9. Martha
11. Mary
14. Judas
16. Simon
17. Peter
18. Paul
20. Joanna
21. Nathanael
22. Susanna

Down
1. Priscilla
4. Thomas
5. Mary
6. Rhoda
7. James
8. Bartholomew
10. Thaddaeus
12. Andrew
13. Dorcas
15. Salome
17. Philip
19. Barnabas

86

87

you must be born again

88

the Lord's

89

nine cubits (13 feet) long
and four cubits (6 feet) wide

90

Paul

91

wept and kissed her

92

Across
3. Tarsus
5. Stephen
6. Salamis
7. Pisidia
8. Antioch

Down
1. Barnabas
2. Antioch
4. Christians

93

content
little
circumstances
secret
hungry
all
strengthens
OECRUAG
courage

94

NOT SEVEN TIMES, BUT, I TELL YOU,
SEVENTY-SEVEN
TIMES

490

95

Joel

96

the church

97

Across
2. Nehemiah
5. Huldah
7. Elijah
10. Josiah
11. Ezra
12. Amos
13. Micah
14. Micah

Down
1. Micah
3. Huldah
4. Jeremiah
6. Amos
8. Hosea
9. Jeremiah

98

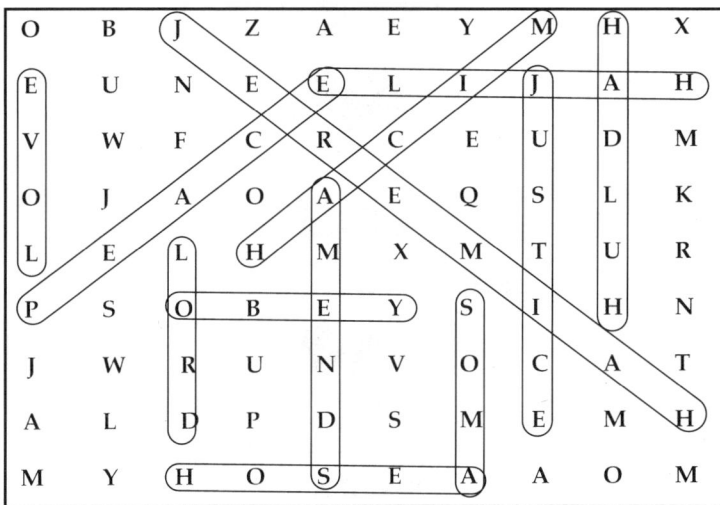

99

"The Hebrew women are different."

100

he was the city treasuer

101

Syria

102

Leah's eyes were lovely, and
Rachel was graceful and beautiful.

103

Solomon

104

throw him into a pit

105

left Peter standing at the door

106

Ramah

107
"How much did you receive for the land?"

108
Abraham

109
faith

110
Simeon
Messiah
Spirit
Temple
Mary
Joseph
Jesus
praised
salvation
Anna
praise

111
purple

112
three

113
Abram

114
news of their faith and love

115
yes, his mind could not rest

116
Tryphosa

117
was Paul's co-worker in Christ

118
all the king's servants

119
Judah

120
married foreign women

121
sent her into exile

122
Naphtali

123
two small coins; all she had

124
pure gold
offering
faith
golden rule
anointing oil
wine, myrrh
myrrh, aloes
stacte, onycha, galbanum, frankincense
holy, Lord
covenant

125
living water

126
180

127

Rejoice in the Lord always.

128

He lost his voice.

129

Josiah (He was king of Judah.)

130

"Take courage, for I am with you."

131

He helped her water her sheep.